Little Dog, Big Dog

JOHN RUBISCH

Illustrated by JENNIFER ERRICKSON

This book is dedicated to

Scruffy McDuffy and Link

for their source of inspiration during many

long walks in the park.

See Big Dog catch the disk at

youtu.be/K05LAG5lFEk

"Sally! Sally! Look what I have," said Daddy.

"It's a little dog!" said Sally.
"Now we have two dogs.
Big Dog and Little Dog!"

Sally and her father took Big Dog and Little Dog
to the park. When they got to the park,
they would take the dogs off their leashes.

The dogs loved to race.

"Go, Big Dog!" shouted Sally.
"Go, Little Dog!"

Big Dog would always win.

Then Daddy would throw the disk.

"Yeah for Big Dog! He caught the disk," shouted Sally. "Can we see if Little Dog will catch the disk?"

"OK," said Daddy.
He threw the disk, but Little Dog
just stared at it and did not move.

"Maybe Little Dog will have to watch Big Dog a few more times to learn how to catch the disk," said Daddy.

On Thursday nights, the family would put the trash out for the garbage truck. Big Dog always helped by carrying out a box for recycling.

"Look!" said Sally.
"Little Dog is trying to help!"

"Yes," said Daddy.
"But the box is just too big for him.
He'll learn as he gets older."

Day after day,
Sally would play with
Big Dog and Little Dog
and they would have lots of fun.

One day they went to the park. Daddy said, "Big Dog is slowing down. He's getting old."

As always, when they got to the park, the dogs began to race. But this time… Little Dog won! "Yeah for Little Dog!" cheered Sally. "He won!"

Daddy was not cheering.
He was looking at Big Dog.

"Big Dog is limping,"
he said. "We better
take him to see the vet."

Daddy, Sally, and Big Dog
went to see Dr. Smith,
the animal doctor.

Dr. Smith looked at Big Dog.
Big Dog seemed sad.

She said to Daddy, "Mr. Johnson,
can I talk to you alone?"

Daddy and Dr. Smith left the room.
"Don't worry, Big Dog," Sally said. "Dr. Smith will
give you some medicine and you'll be all better."

Daddy came back in the room.
He said, "I have some bad news, Sally.
Big Dog is in a lot of pain. He hurts
really bad. Dr. Smith is going to have
to put Big Dog into a special kind of sleep."

"Sleep?" said Sally. "When will he get up?"

"He won't," said Daddy. "We'll leave Big
Dog here with Dr. Smith and he will sleep
for a very LONG time."

"No!" screamed Sally.
"I want to take Big Dog home!"

"If we take Big Dog home, he'll be in a lot of pain," said Daddy. "He'll always hurt and he won't get better. If he goes to sleep, he won't feel the hurt."

Sally sat quietly. Then she said,
"I don't want Big Dog to hurt.
He should go to sleep."

She threw her arms around
Big Dog's neck and started to cry.

"I love you, Big Dog.
I'm going to miss you.
But you stay and go to sleep."

When they got to the park,
Sally said, "Big Dog is not here,
but can you throw the disk?"

Daddy threw the disk.

Suddenly, Little Dog ran toward the disk! He jumped, and flew through the air...

...and caught the disk in his mouth!

"Little Dog caught the disk!" screamed Sally excitedly.

"Yes!" said Daddy. "It seems that Little Dog was watching Big Dog and learned how to catch the disk himself."

When it was Thursday night, Sally said, "Let's get Little Dog to take the recycling out."

Sally found a small box and said, "Come on, Little Dog. You can do it just like Big Dog."

Little Dog just stared at the box.
Then... he grabbed it by his teeth
and took it out for recycling!

"Yeah!" said Sally, clapping her hands. "Little Dog learned from Big Dog how to take out the box!"

"I guess he did!" laughed Daddy.

One day Daddy came home and said, "Sally, Sally! Look what I have."

"It's a new dog," said Sally.
"Now we have two dogs again,
Little Dog and New Dog!
And Little Dog will teach New Dog
everything he learned from Big Dog!"

Acknowledgments

Thanks to Angela Reisinger, Shauna Haley and Shannon Wevodau and their children for reading and reviewing this book before publication. Thanks to Earline Bellaman for her continuous constructive feedback throughout. Thanks to Jennifer Errickson for her patience and skill in bringing Little Dog and Big Dog to life. –JCR

Email jcr1377@rocketmail.com
https://christophersstory.net

 Year of the Book
135 Glen Ave.
Glen Rock, PA 17327

Softcover ISBN: 978-1-64649-122-3
Hardcover ISBN: 978-1-64649-123-0

Library of Congress Control Number: 2020919867

About the Author

John Rubisch is a retired high school counselor. His previous works are *Christopher's Story: An Indictment of the American Mental Health System* and *Mill River Senior High.*

About the Illustrator

Jennifer Errickson lives in York, Pennsylvania with her husband who is also an artist, and their four-year-old son. She received her Associates Degree in Art/ Illustration from Pennsylvania College of Art and Design in 2000. She has always had a passion for the visual arts, and motherhood has inspired her to pursue her lifelong dream of illustrating children's books.

CPSIA information can be obtained
at www.ICGtesting.com
Printed in the USA
LVHW060813011220
672994LV00004B/18

9 781646 491230